John Bellinger

An inaugural dissertation on chronic pneumony,

Or pulmonary consumption : submitted to the examination of the Rev.

John Ewing, S.T.P. provost ; the trustees & medical faculty, of the

University of Pennsylvania, on the sixth day of June, 1799

John Bellinger

An inaugural dissertation on chronic pneumony,
*Or pulmonary consumption : submitted to the examination of the Rev. John Ewing,
S.T.P. provost ; the trustees & medical faculty, of the University of Pennsylvania, on
the sixth day of June, 1799*

ISBN/EAN: 9783337730284

Printed in Europe, USA, Canada, Australia, Japan

Cover: Foto ©ninafisch / pixelio.de

More available books at **www.hansebooks.com**

AN

INAUGURAL DISSERTATION

ON

CHRONIC PNEUMONY,

OR

Pulmonary Confumption:

SUBMITTED TO

THE EXAMINATION

OF THE

REV. JOHN EWING, S. T. P. PROVOST;

THE

TRUSTEES & MEDICAL FACULTY,

OF THE

UNIVERSITY OF PENNSYLVANIA,

On the fixth Day of June, 1799,

FOR THE DEGREE OF

DOCTOR OF MEDICI.

———————

By JOHN SKOTTOWE BELLINGER,
Of Charleston, South Carolina,
MEMBER OF THE PHILADELPHIA MEDICAL AND CHEMICAL SOCIETIES.

———————

BENJAMIN RUSH, M. D.

PROFESSOR OF THE INSTITUTES AND OF CLINICAL MEDICINE,

IN THE

UNIVERSITY OF PENNSYLVANIA.

MUCH RESPECTED SIR,

HAVING enjoyed, for nearly four years, thofe great advantages infeparably connected with being your pupil, it would be a dereliction of that gratitude fo much your due, did I refrain from expreffing my acknowledgments upon the prefent occafion.

I beg you, therefore, to confider this effay as a tribute of gratitude ; and to receive the warmeft wifhes for your health, happinefs, and long continued fuccefs in the fcience of medicine, of

Your greatly indebted
Pupil and Friend,
J. S. BELLINGER.

TO

PIERCE BUTLER, Esq.

DEAR SIR,

PERMIT me thus publicly to acknowledge my obligations to you for the friendship and polite attention I have received from yourself and amiable family, during my residence in Philadelphia; and at the same time to express the great respect I have always entertained for your public and private character.

With sentiments of high esteem,

I remain your much obliged,

And grateful Friend,

J. S. BELLINGER.

INAUGURAL DISSERTATION, &c.

———

THE subject which I have chosen for the following differtation, is Chronic Pneumony, or Pulmonary Confumption. This difeafe ufually commences with the fymptoms of a common cold, flight ftitches in the fides and breaft, fome degree of fever, pain in the head, back, joints, and limbs. To thefe may be added a difficulty of breathing, and flight cough,* troublefome only at night. The above fymptoms are frequently fo flight, as to give no indication of danger to the patient; from which caufe they are feldom attended to, and foon become aggravated—the cough becomes more apparent, and fomewhat diftreffing, and is, as yet, not accom-

---

* Cough, though a very general, is, by no means, a neceffary confequence of a pulmonary difeafe. Dr. *Rufh* takes notice of this, and gives the hiftory and the appearances on diffection of a young lady who died of this difeafe without the above fymptom. *Bonetus* in his *Sepulcretum* has alfo the diffection of a woman, in whom a large fchirrus of the fize of an egg was found in the right lobe of the lungs: this patient had laboured long under a fever; but had never had a cough.

panied with any difcharge; the nights are paffed in a more reftlefs manner;—pains more acute and fixed are now felt in the thorax; refpiration hurried and performed with more difficulty—fome frothy mucus is now expectorated, fmall in quantity, tough, and ropy, with much difficulty, which fenfibly relieves the oppreffion for a fhort period. The pulfe is generally, at this period of the difeafe, hard and full; but fometimes quick and irregular.

At the firft appearance of the above fymptoms, the tongue is white and the countenance pale,—appetite impaired, and the ftomach weak, often rejecting food. This difpofition to vomit, when accompanied with a cough, *Morton* confiders as a certain Pathagnomonic fymptom of a pulmonary affection. While phthifis is in this fimple ftate, the patient goes about and imagines no dangerous confequences will enfue from thefe feemingly trifling fymptoms. This ftate of things often remains ftationary for weeks, though not unfrequently the fever foon increafes, and an exacerbation takes place in the afternoon of every day. All the other fymptoms are now increafed, and perfpiration breaks out, in the morning, upon the upper part of the body, but, more particularly, on the breaft and forehead. When this takes place a remiffion of all the feverifh fymptoms foon enfues, and continues throughout the fore part of the day. The cough, which has been gradually increaſing, in violence and frequency, is aggravated by a recumbent poſture of the body—prevents ſleep and diſtreſſes the patient, till the diſcharge of the morning ſweat takes place, to his great joy : as he now feels that repoſe and eaſe which had been long wiſhed for in vain. The matter of expectoration is frequently ſtreaked with blood, and daily increaſes in quantity. When the exacerbation of fever is at its height, a redneſs of the cheeks, lips, and tongue, is perceived.— The fever is heightened after eating, more particularly, of ſolids ; and, after much exerciſe, fluſhings of the face and a ſenſation of heat in the hands and feet, are experienced. As the diſeaſe advances, the fever is more fixed, and the remiſſion more perceptible. It begins about noon, continues to increaſe till evening, and laſts the greater part of the night, when the patient is again relieved by the diſcharge of ſweat. But it occaſionally occurs, that this paroxyſm of fever remits early in the afternoon, and after this, a ſecond exacerbation enſues, which is alſo relieved by the diſcharge of perſpiration. This ſecond paroxyſm, however, appears to be an adventitious occurrence, produced by occaſional circumſtances.

After ſuch reſtleſs nights, the patient, as might be expected, is weak, languid, and not at all refreſhed by the little ſleep, which he uſually enjoys towards morning. The pulfe is quicker than when in health; yet, it can eafily be perceived, that a remiffion has taken place, as well from the ftate of his pulfe, as his own fenfations. The expectoration, which has hitherto been fmall in quantity, is now much in-creafed, and in the morning is combined with *pus*, in round maffes, fometimes difagreeable to the tafte, of a yellow, greenifh, and, as the difeafe advances, of a dirty brown colour. The pain in the breaft generally abates in violence as the expectoration be-comes thinner: for, from this circumftance, the lungs are lefs agitated, although the cough be lefs frequent. The quantity of urine is more diminifhed than when in health, is high coloured and depofits a brown or white fediment.

The difeafe appears to be now confirmed: tho' the matter coughed up be fmall in quantity. From a continuance of the above fymptoms, and from their increafe, in violence, the body gives ftriking proofs of decay: the fat, which, in health, fills the fockets of the eyes, now difappears, and they fink, become weak, dull and languid—the cheeks are high and prominent—the flefh waftes gradually away from every part of the body—the nofe ap-pears thin and fharp—the temples are depreffed, and the ftrength daily fails.

The pulfe in phthifis is fometimes *Synoca, Synocus,*

Synocula, *Hectic*, and *Typhus*.* The two laft ftates
of the pulfe, do not always occur in the laft ftage
of this difeafe. The appetite, from the very commencement of confumption, is lefs impaired than
we would expect, and often continues good until
the near approach of diffolution : it is even frequently very keen, and, as this is a favouable occurrence in moft difeafes of long continuance, we
muft be careful in not being deceived by it, and
haftily prognofticate returning health. I have obferved one or two inftances, in which phthifical
patients appeared to have no defire for food; but,
within a few days of their death, their appetites became exceffive, and continued in this morbid ftate,
until that event took place. Coftivenefs is ufually
a conftant fymptom of confumption in its beginning, particularly, after the morning perfpiration
commences. From the febrile fymptoms being increafed towards the afternoon, and the expectoration lefs in quantity, the patient is afflicted with an
intolerable anxiety at the breaft, which is aggravated by the obftructed veffels of the lungs, refifting the paffage of the increafed circulation of blood

---

* A *Synoca* pulfe is feldom very quick, but full and hard.
A *Synocus* is quick and full but not hard. *Synocula*, is quick
and tenfe attended with a jirk and fmall volume. The *Hectic*
is full, frequent, and fometimes hard ; and the *Typhus* is weak,
quick and irregular without hardnefs.

RUSH's LECTURES.

through them. We cannot be furprifed at this occurring to fo great a degree in this ftate in the above vifcus, fince we perceive the fame effect enfue even in the found ftate of the lungs, from an increafed circulation, by any caufe, either of exercife or of fever.

About this period of the difeafe in the *fair fex*, the menftrual difcharge ufually ceafes:—it however fometimes occurs at an earlier period; and, whenever this ceffation takes place, it never fails of cherifhing that delufive hope, which feems to be almoft peculiar to this difeafe; and which often continues, to within a few days of death. The above occurrence uniformly appears to be convincing to the minds of the patients and their friends, as the fole caufe of all the fymptoms that enfue after its ceffation. But although the menftrual flux ufually ceafes in a fhort time after the attack of phthifis; yet, there are cafes on record, in which it has occurred at its ftated periods, and continued regular during the whole continuance of a lingering difeafe.

When the fuppreffion of the menfes enfues, practitioners ought to be careful left they be alfo deceived; and by directing their whole attention to this *one* fymptom, thus lofe the beft and perhaps the only opportunity, they may poffefs, of affording the unfortunate patient a chance of recovery.

A diarrhea is ufually, though not certainly, one of the laft fymptoms of the difeafe; but we fometimes meet with a few cafes of phthifis in which this fymptom never occurs. A purging however not unfrequently appears in an early ftage. When diarrhea takes place, patients are relieved from that anxiety and oppreffion, which had hitherto diftreffed them; and the pyrexia, burning at the breaft, and fweating at night, abate. As the purging increafes, the fever and expectoration diminifh, the ftrength rapidly declines; fo that they are fcarcely able to move without much fatigue. When phthifis is far advanced, patients can fcarcely articulate their words: in attempting which, pain is produced and a difpofition to cough enfues. This is attended with a remarkably hollow found very diftreffing to a by-ftander. Even in this ftage of things, the poor patient ftill flatters himfelf with the idea of a reco-very, particularly if the defire for food be prefent; which is unfortunately too often the cafe. The memory is fo much difeafed that patients feldom recollect the occurrences of the preceding day:—and I have obferved, in two cafes, the fenfe of hearing to be much impaired. In the above patients I could not attribute the deafnefs to any other caufe than the difeafe. They both died.

In the clofe of confumption frequent convulfions and dyfpnœa take place: the cough and alfo the expectoration greatly diminifh, owing to the inability of the patient in making the exertion neceffary to the difcharge of the latter : as the pus fticks in the trachia, the difficulty of refpiration is increafed and fometimes this function is fufpended. Matter is occafionally expectorated with little or no exertion or coughing. In fome cafes, an acute pain in the breaft, which is increafed by the cough, or a tenfion or pain when patients lie upon the right or left fide, produces a quick, hurried, and diftreffing refpiration, and even ftops it for a time. This is alfo produced by tubercles preffing upon the unobftructed bronchial veffels. If, from either accident or defign, the diarrhea be ftopped in any period of confumption, the fever, anxiety and diftrefs of the patient are greatly increafed. I once faw this circumftance occur in a young man three or four days before his death, and he continued coftive until that event took place, though laxative medicines were adminiftered. The great difpofition to fweat, which having once taken place, is a conftant fymptom, is diminifhed and fometimes ceafes, towards the clofe of the difeafe. When confumption is far advanced, the patient lies on his back, with his head and fhoulders raifed high by pillows ; but in an earlier ftage, his pofture is in moft inftances on the affected fide. The evacuations by ftool, are extremely fœtid, and are faid to be often white, but this appearance I have never feen. The breath

generally becomes very difagreeable, more particularly when death is near at hand.

Together with the preceding fymptoms, the legs,
feet, and hands occafionally fwell ; and the patient
being now weak, low and emaciated, has a frequent, diftreffing hiccough, profufe fweats, foul
tongue, low voice, and convulfions—and death
foon clofes the fcene in fome cafes : while in
others, the wretched patient continues his mifera-
ble exiftence for weeks. Hippocrates fays that a
falling off of the hair is a fymptom of impending
death. This fymptom is by no means conftant,
for it does not always occur even in flow confumptions. The difeafe of which we are treating often
makes a more rapid progrefs. In thefe cafes
the fymptoms are increafed in force, follow each
other in quicker fucceffion ; and, in proportion to
their violence, death takes place in a few weeks,
months, or as many years. We fee cafes recorded
in almoft every writer upon this difeafe, in proof
of its continuing many years ; and Dr. Rufh, in
his lectures, quotes a cafe of phthifis, which began
at the 17th year of age and continued to the 70th.
This diverfity, as to the duration of phthifis, appears to depend upon the habit and mode of life of
the patient, the feafon of the year, and alfo the cli-
mate in which the attack is made, and fome other
occafional circumftances.

When patients are deftroyed after a fhort illnefs, by this complaint, it is denominated a *galloping* confumption.

It is ufual for confumption to make very confiderable progrefs, in the female fex, previous to its being attended to: from this circumftance alone, fhould they not be regarded with the greateft circumfpection, upon the flighteft appearance of its fymptoms, left, through neglect, the difeafe be permitted to take fo ftrong a hold of the conftitution, as to render all exertions fruitlefs? When pregnancy takes place, in any ftage of phthifis, a fufpenfion of all the fymptoms moft ufually enfues. This flattering deception continues until delivery, when they return, for the moft part, in a violent manner, and foon prove fatal. From confumption almoft uniformly being arrefted, in its progrefs, by conception, this circumftance has attracted the notice of many authors; and as it is the foundation of the ingenious theory of an eminent writer, will be confidered in a more proper place. I muft not omit mentioning, however, that this ftate of the fyftem is not the only occurrence that fufpends the progrefs of this dreadful difeafe. It alternates " with mania, diarrhea dyfentery, dyfpepfia, and rheumatifm."* Mania feizing the patient has frequently

* Rufh's Lectures.

protracted the death of confumptive perfons, even when far advanced in the difeafe. Dr. Mead relates the following cafe of a young lady, who, after having been troubled with a violent cough and fpitting of blood, for two months, was attacked with a hectic, attended with thirst, heat and night fweats, together with great wasting of flesh, and frequent fpitting of tough slime from the lungs and throat, interfperfed here and there with fmall portions of yellow purulent matter. From a certain caufe she was now feized with religious madnefs; from which time the fymptoms of the original difeafe began to abate : the febrile heat decreafed, the fpitting stopped, the fweats diminished, and the bodily strength feemed to become more adequate to performing the functions of life, in proportion as the mind grew lefs capable of governing the body. In a few days, she became melancholy, and about the end of the third month, the hectic and ulceration returning, she finally died.

The above is the ufual termination of fuch cafes; but occafionally phthifis is perfectly cured. Dr. *Cullen* exprefsly remarks that a mania has fometimes entirely cured this difeafe. Dr. *Rufh* in his 2d vol. informs us, that three clinical patients, in the Pennfylvania Hofpital, in the winter of 1772, were relieved *feveral times* of a cough by pains in their limbs; and, as *often*, the pains in their limbs feemed for a while to promife a cure to their pulmonic complaints. Many confumptive perfons were relieved, and fome recovered, according to Dr. *Blane*, in confequence of the terror excited by the hurricane, which took place at *Barbadoes* in 1780. Dr. *Bennet*, in his treatife on the nature and cure of confumptions, mentions the cafe of a phthifical patient, who was attacked with a violent pain in the teeth for two days, and in whom, during that time, every fymptom of confumption, except the leannefs of the body, altogether vanifhed. The fame author adds alfo, that a defluxion on the lungs, had often been relieved by falivary evacuations.

Dr. Thunburg, in his travels, after relating the accident which happened on board his veffel, from a quantity of white lead having been ufed in frying fome pancakes, informs us, that the captain fuffered much from a colic, which continued violent for two days: the Doctor then obferves, " he was of a confumptive habit, and his cough kept away for *feveral* days in confequence of this accident."

Perfons of tender, weak and delicate conftitutions, particularly thofe poffeffing narrow and flat chefts, prominent fhoulders, and long necks, are moft ufually the fubjects of phthifis. Thofe perfons conftantly occupied in certain manufactories are often afflicted with this difeafe. Dr. *Kirkland* obferves, " that fcythe-grinders are fubject to a difeafe of the lungs, from the particles of fand mixing with iron-duft, which among themfelves, they call the *grinders' rot.*" It is faid that perfons of a delicate, thin and fair complexion, and thofe who have grown rapidly, are moft liable to this difeafe. Many authors fuppofe, that white and tranfparent teeth, are characteriftics of a predifpofition to pulmonary confumption. Dr. *Simmons* afferts, that the greater number of thofe who are carried off by this complaint, will be found never to have had a carious tooth. From the fmall experience I have had, it is impoffible to give an opinion; but it is certain, many are afflicted with this difeafe who have bad teeth.

Females are oftener attacked with phthifis than males. This appears to arife, in part, from their more fedentary lives, the ftructure of their bodies, and alfo, from their thorax being more confined by their manner of drefs. From the laft caufe, the ribs muft be depreffed, the thorax ftraitened, the abdomen compreffed, the action of the diaphragm greatly impeded, and thus fuch a formation of body is often induced, as to indicate a difpofition to difeafes of the breaft. It is to the above caufe, *Spigelius* afcribes the frequency of phthifis in England: he remarks, that, " that folicitude which young

women fhew to make themfelves appear *taper-fhaped*
is abfurd and incredibly pernicious; for whilft, by
ftays, and other hurtful contrivances, they ftrait-
en their chefts, they do not confider that they are
preparing the way for confumptions, and decays."
This complaint occurs in perfons of every age,
even from infancy to an advanced period of life;
but from puberty to about thirty-fix, at which time
the human body has attained its *acme*, it makes its
greateft ravages. The Indians are believed to be
exempted from this difeafe. But, as in many books
confumption of the lungs is enumerated among their
common difeafes, I was defirous to obtain more
accurate information upon the fubject. Accordingly
I made application to Dr. *Barton*, who, from his
attention to the *natural hiftory* of thefe people, I
expected could fatisfy me upon this point. In a
converfation I lately had with the Doctor, he informed me, that the Indians were often afflicted with
confumption; and that he had feen cafes of it in
his travels among them in the ftate of *New York*.
The Doctor added, alfo, that he had proofs of
phthifis being among the Indians previous to their
much intercourfe with the *whites*: although more
prevalent with them now than formerly. He then
very politely favoured me with the following extract
of a letter he had received from Mr. *James Geddes*,
a refpectable gentleman refiding at *Onondago Lake*
in the ftate of *New York*, dated the 16th of No-

vember, 1798. " The Indians here decreafe. Three years ago, there were 133, and laft *spring* when they received their money, there were but 105. They almoft all die of the 'phthifis pulmonalis." Dr. *Barton* further remarked, that the above was but one among many facts, in his poffeffion, of the exiftence of confumption in thefe people. I muft add however that thefe *Onondago* Indians do not live as they formerly did; which fhews, in a confpicuous manner, the influence of certain modes of life upon the human body in producing difeafes. Dr. Rufh obferves, " that it is fcarcely known by thofe citizens of the United States, who live in the *firft* ftage of civilized life, and who have lately obtained the title of the *firft fettlers.*" The inhabitants of large and populous towns are more frequently fufferers by this difeafe, than thofe who refide in the country. We may add alfo, that the Negroes in South Carolina, who purfue an active life, are rarely the victims of confumption.

From the authority of nearly all writers, we may affert phthifis pulmonalis to be an hereditary difeafe. It has been obferved in contradiction to this, that, as by proper precautions, the unfortunate defcendant may efcape the difeafe of his anceftors, confumption is not, ftrictly fpeaking, an hereditary complaint. But the fame objection applies with equal force to other difeafes, which are allowed to be hereditary. Gout may be noticed as an example. Perfons who are thus predifpofed to phthifis, are remarked to have the fymptoms in a flow and gradual manner, and hold out much longer, though death is more frequently the iffue, than when the difeafe occurs without this ftate of the fyftem.

Confumption is faid by many authors to be *contagious*; but although we find cafes in proof of this, related by *Van Swieten, Darwin* and other writers of the firft reputation, I fhould rather attribute the attack of the difeafe, to the great want of exercife, and the impure air the perfons breathe who attend the fick; and alfo to a family predifpofition, when it occurs in the relations of the deceafed. The Baron Van Swieten fuppofes fome danger might arife from the breath of the fick, though the fpittle be not very fœtid: to prove this, he gives us the following extraordinary hiftory. " A man's wife, expiring of a confumption, gave him a farewel kifs. All that part of his chin, which her lips had touched, remained ever after *fmooth*, although the beard grew thick all around." Phthifical perfons are fenfibly affected by every change of the weather, particularly a fudden tranfition from heat to cold. It is obferved that the air on fea fhores, is detrimental to thofe afflicted with this difeafe; but when at fea they are much benefited. In this cafe, the effects produced feem to arife from the mixture of the fea and land atmof-phere.

The matter fpit up, in pulmonary complaints, varies in all refpects, according to the period of the difeafe; and as by fome it is fuppofed that, from an attentive examination of it, we may draw indications, from its appearance, of the effects of the *mode* of cure, which has been purfued, we may, to fatify the patient and his friends, daily ex-amine the expectoration. At the commencement of phthifis, the matter of expectoration confifts of only *mucus*, from the trachea, containing much *air*, which may be rendered fenfible by placing it in an inverted glafs, full of water. After fome time the mucus being diffolved, the air is feen rifing in fmall bubbles to the furface of the water. At a certain period of the difeafe, various in different patients, *pus* appears in the matter coughed up. This in-creafes daily in quantity, is of a brown, dirty co-lour, tinged green or with blood, of a globular form, often fœtid, and fometimes fweet to the tafte.

We will now mention fome of the tefts to diftin-guifh thefe two fluids from each other; though I muft confefs, the knowledge we may poffefs, rela-tive to this criterion, appears to be no great acquifition in the cure of the complaint. Pus, when agitated in water, is foon mixed with it, and on remaining at reft, for fome hours, a precipitate will take place. But no precipitate enfues from the union of water and mucus, which is more difficultly effected than that of pus and water. When pus is put into water it finks; but mucus fwims on its furface. From thefe circumftances, however, no inferences fhould be immediately made of the matter fpit up, being either pus or mucus, becaufe the former fometimes finks and the latter often fwims: —the one, occafioned by its being expectorated in lumps—the other, from its containing air or being greatly blended with mucus. As the above is not unfrequently the cafe, we fhould not form an opinion until the matter be agitated fome time.

The following experiments are confidered to be more conclufive. Let the expectorated matter be diffolved in fulphuric acid, or a folution of cauftic alkali, then add pure water. If there be a fair precipitation in each folution, it is certain that fome *pus* is prefent. But if this does not occur, it is a fure teft that the matter is entirely mucus. If the matter cannot be made to diffolve in the alkaline lixivium there is alfo reafon to believe that it is *pus*. I have often tried the above modes of difcovering the nature of the expectoration of perfons labouring under confumption, but with fo little variation

from the above, which I have collected from authors, that it is unneceffary to particularife them.
It is proper to examine what is expectorated during
the night and morning only, and that alfo which is
brought up by a flight cough without much ftrain-
ing. This is neceffary even in the advanced ftage of
phthifis, as, during the day, when the patient has
difcharged much pus in the night by coughing, he
expectorates very little elfe than mucus.

The late unfortunate and ingenious Dr. Stark
fuppofed, that the fpittings of confumptive perfons
differed both from *mucus* and *pus*. The Doctor
found it to be more eafily diffufible in water than
mucus, and at firft forming a permanent ropy fluid,
but in a few days depofiting a fediment in the fame
manner as pus does: the liquor, however, ftill continuing ropy, refembling mucus and water. The
above appearance I have never obferved, though I
particularly attended to it in two patients who were
far advanced in the difeafe. Perhaps Dr. Stark
might have been mifled by not carefully feparating
the two fluids from each other, before he made
his experiments; for as fome mucus is almoft uni-
verfally combined with pus in the expectoration of
patients, this may have been the caufe of the apparent difference which he obferved. When the
expectoration is very fœtid, it is fuppofed, by many
authors, to indicate a mortification; but this ap-

pears to be a hafty conclufion, as there are many inftances on record, in which perfons have lived years while labouring under this fymptom, and fome have even recovered after this has been the cafe to a great degree. Van Swieten records the cafe of a youth who fpat much fœtid matter in the morning: he had been afflicted with confumption for a long time previous to this fœtid matter being difcharged, and he lived two years after its appearance.

We will next confider the appearances upon diffection. In the cellular fubftance of the lungs, are found bodies of a roundifh figure, firm confiftence, and of various fizes, from half an inch in diameter to the fmalleft fize, that are called *tubercles.* The fmall ones are always folid. Many of the large tubercles are obferved together, often hard, their colour fomewhat white, and fimilar to cartilage. Their furface, when cut through, appears fmooth, fhining and uniform. In fome are obferved one or more fmall holes; but in others fmall cavities filled with a fluid like pus. At the bottom of thefe cavities, fmall holes are often feen, which upon being preffed, difcharge matter. Thefe holes do not appear to have communication with any veffels. The cavities of tubercles are, in fome, from half to three-fourths of an inch in fize; but in others, they are barely perceptible. The larger ones, when cut and emptied, refemble fmall white cups, nothing remaining of the fubftance of the tubercle except a thin covering or capfula. Thofe cavities fmaller than half an inch are always fhut; but thofe larger have a round opening made by a branch of the tra- chæa. Dr. Stark, from whom this hiftory is taken, could not obferve on the cut furface of the fmall tubercles, either cells, veficles, or veffels, even when examined with a microfcope, after injecting the pulmonary artery and vein. Tubercles are fel- dom found without adhefions of the lungs to the Pleura. The confiftence of the contents of the tu- bercles, often differs in the fame fubject: thus, while fome contain a fluid, others are filled with a thick fubftance of the nature of frefh cheefe. When there exifts an opening from the tubercles in- to the trachæa, and by this a communication be- tween them and the external air, they have been denominated *vomicæ*; which now come under con- fideration.

The large vomicæ are of an oval form, lined with a fmooth and tender membrane, and are moft commonly ruptured. When many of thefe are fituated near each other, they form large ulcers. The fmall vomicæ, are not often found ruptured. We find openings to exift between the larger vomi- cæ from one to the other: thefe canals are irregu- lar and not fmooth. Several openings are alfo per- ceived into large vomicæ by the bronchial ramifications; but thefe are round and fmooth. The fluid, found in vomicæ, previous to a rupture, is white and fomewhat yellow; but after this has taken place, it is *red*. If not perfectly broken we find the fluid to be rarely red, but of a yellowifh colour, fometimes brown and often fœtid. The above fluids are diffu- fible in water whether the vomicæ be ruptured or not. The fituation of large vomicæ is ufually in the back parts of the upper lobes, but we find them in all parts of the lungs, although moft frequently on their external furface. *Valfalva*, who diffected many confumptive perfons, found the ulcer and dif- eafe in almoft all his cafes upon the upper part of the lungs. Thofe parts of the lungs near the cir- cumference of the vomicæ, are found inflamed, fomewhat hard and impervious to air when blown in the trachæa. The contiguous parts of the lungs are often foft, tending to fuppuration. Thofe blood- veffels near the large vomicæ are much contracted in their circumference, and though they may ap- pear as large as thofe which communicate with parts of the lungs not difeafed, yet their diameters are nearly clofed with a fibrous fubftance.

After having injected the arteries and veins of a difeafed lung, Dr. Stark, upon cutting into the founder parts, faw numberlefs ramuli filled with the wax; but no fuch appearance could he difcover in the difeafed portions. The veffels of the trachæa which open into the vomicæ are found in their internal furface to be inclining to red, but of their natural fize. The liver has been difcovered to be hard and indurated. The pancreas and fpleen have been likewife found to be difeafed; and the villous coat of the inteftines has often, after a long continued purging, exhibited marks of erofion.

In fome cafes of phthifis, the fubftance of the lungs have been found nearly all deftroyed; and we often fee one-half confumed, though in common, about one-third or one-fourth only is deftroyed. Dr. *Haller* found, inftead of the left lobe of the lungs (which had entirely difappeared) a great quantity of almoft fœtid water vifcid like the white of an egg. In *Bonetus*, we have the cafe of a woman, in whom both lobes of the lungs were entirely purulent. In the fame book is alfo the diffection of an infant boy, who died of this difeafe, in whom there was no veftige of the left lung or the pleura; and a large abfcefs was found in the *mediaftinum*. Thefe different appearances, with refpect to the quantity of the lungs found difeafed, feem to be produced in proportion to the violence of the morbid action, and not to the duration of the difeafe. In thofe deftroyed by a violent and hafty confumption, the lungs exhibit more evident figns of deftruction than in thofe, whofe difeafes have been of long duration, and attended with lefs violent fymptoms. That a fuppuration might take place without confuming the part from whence it arifes, appears to have been firft noticed by the late Dr. *Hunter*. This fometimes happens in pulmonary confumption. The lungs have been difcovered found, although much pus had been expeftorated during life. A remarkable inftance of this is recorded by *De Haen* to have taken place in the hofpital at Vienna: he found the lungs of a perfon, who had difcharged a very great quantity of pus by fpitting, entire. When cut into, not a drop of pus, nor the leaft marks of a vomicæ were to be difcovered. Some pus was in the trachæa. Upon the diffeftion of a man who had difcharged much blood before his death, Dr. *Simfon* difcovered a fchirrus upon the upper part of the right lobe and a finus filled with pus. The left lobe of the lungs was without hardnefs, well coloured and appeared found. He was however much furprifed to fee *pus* iffue from every part of its furface when cut, and this *too*, in different places.

Both lobes of the lungs are fometimes difeafed, but moft frequently only one. In the opinion of moft authors, who have had the greateft opportunities of judging, the *left* lobe is moft frequently affefted. May not this arife from the left pulmonary artery being *fhorter* than the right? And thus, would it not receive a greater impulfe in circulation?

No other remarkable appearances are difcovered upon diffection, other than that the lymphatic glands of the cheft have been found of a dark co-lour, containing a white fubftance of the confiftence of pafte.

We now proceed to the confideration of the *caufes* of confumption. The caufes of *difeafe* have been divided into *remote*, *predifpofing*, *exciting*, and *proximate*: upon each of which I fhall fay a few words in their proper order.

The *remote* caufes of this difeafe are fuch, as by their action upon the whole fyftem, or the lungs particularly, render them more fufceptible of the impreffion of ftimuli by inducing *debility*. This is of two fpecies, according as the caufe be either fti-mulating or the reverfe. .Thefe caufes may be di-vided into *local* and *general*: the former acting up-on the lungs *directly*, the latter *indirectly* through the medium of the whole body.

The *local* caufes, which I fhall firft confider, ap-pear to be hœmoptyfis, wounds of the lungs, or difcharges of matter into them, in confequence of other ftates of difeafe, bruifes and falls injuring the thorax, and the duft difcharged in certain manufac-tories. A fpitting of blood is fuppofed by many to be the moft general caufe of confumption. The

teftimony of many authors of great refpectability
and daily obfervation, prove this to be entirely erro-
neous. Many perfons not only have phthifis without this precurfor, but numbers have this fymptom
for years, and who have lived to an advanced age
free from confumption. In every medical record,
we have examples to prove the above affertions.
When it occurs in perfons liable to this difeafe from
an hereditary predifpofition, or any other ftate of
the fyftem, it is, however, very frequently followed by phthifis. An ill-cured pleurify or peripneu-
mony is often the caufe of confumption. It appears to be natural to fuppofe that wounds of the
lungs would be always fucceeded by this difeafe; but
the reverfe is ufually the cafe. Mr. *John Hunter*,
who certainly poffeffed a very great opportunity of
obtaining accurate information on this fubject, from
his extenfive practice in wounds, in general, in
fpeaking of confumption from wounds of the lungs,
obferves, " I cannot fay I ever faw a cafe where
fuch an effect took place." All phyficians, however, have not been fo fortunate as Mr. Hunter,
fince cafes from this caufe have occafionally been
met with. The principal reafons why we do not
more frequently fee phthifis induced by the above
caufes are, 1ft, From the perfons not being in a ftate
of predifpofition; and, 2dly, From the treatment
that is ufually followed when fuch accidents occur.
I am confident, if an incipient confumption was

always treated in the fame manner, it would as certainly be cured.

Perfons much expofed to the duft of certain fubftances, as millers, miners, fkin-dreffers, and others, are often attacked with phthifis. The workers in mines foon fall victims to their bufinefs, partly from being deprived of *pure* air, and the light of the fun; but, more particularly, from the debility that is induced in their lungs. The effluvia which exifts in mines of arfenic, act powerfully in inducing a difpofition to phthifis. *Chaptal* remarks, that " this metal which is very frequently met with in mines caufes the deftruction of a number of workmen who explore them; being very volatile, it forms a duft which affects and deftroys the lungs; and the unhappy miners, after a languifhing life of a few years, all perifh fooner or later." I am acquainted with a young gentleman of this city who is affected with violent dyfpnœa when expofed to the duft which arifes from the grinding of rye meal. It produces alfo repeated *fneezing*, and he is only to be relieved by removing from the caufe. Bruifes and ftrains of the thorax, produce a difpofition to confumption, more frequently than wounds of the lungs themfeves, merely from their being apparently fo trivial as to demand very little attention. According to Dr. *Lind*, out of 360 perfons whom he attended in phthifis, it was induced by falls, bruifes and ftrains received a year or two before its appearance, in *one-fourth* of them. Among thofe caufes, which appear to produce a debility in the lungs, through the medium of the general fyftem, we may enumerate the following.

1ft, Violent exercife. 2dly, An intemperate mode of life, as hard drinking, great eating, and an exceffive indulgence of the venereal appetite. 3dly, Stimulating paffions of the mind. 4thly, Heat, fuddenly fucceeding cold and moift weather. 5thly, A too fedentary life, and a fudden change in the diet from low to high living. 6thly, A fudden diminution or ftoppage of any ufual evacuation, particularly of blood, as *epiftaxis*, *hæmorrhois*, *menfes*, and the *lochia*. 7thly, A neglect of cuftomary blood-letting, in full habits, and an intemperate ufe of *tobacco*. To the above, I think, may be added the difappearance of certain *eruptions*, which are often obferved upon the *fhoulders* and *breafts* of young perfons, and alfo a non-conformity, in the drefs, to the changes of the weather.

I now proceed to offer a few remarks upon fome of the above caufes, that appear to be moft frequently fucceeded by the effect which is attributed to them. And firft of an intemperate life.

The alluring and tranfitory pleafures of diffipa-

tion, and its concomitants, exclufive of their bane-
ful effects upon the *minds* of its followers, almoft
certainly produce many fatal difeafes of the body ;
of which confumptions are the moft frequent. We
meet with cafes of phthifis, in many *authors*, that
are juftly attributed to the above caufe ; and all
practitioners, of even moderate experience, muft
have obferved the fame. Late hours, hard drinking, and an exceffive exercife of the paffions, feldom fail of inducing *that ftate* of the fyftem, which
predifpofes to phthifis, *even* in thofe, whom other-
wife we might conclude not liable to its attack.
How much more pofitively, then, will this difeafe
fucceed thefe caufes, in perfons predifpofed to phthifis : and how careful, therefore, fhould perfons fo
circumftanced be of themfelves, from the certainty,
that the difeafe is more readily induced in them than
in others ?

2dly, Heat, fuddenly fucceeding cold and moift
weather, violent exercife, ftimulating paffions of
the mind, and a fudden tranfition in diet, from
low to generous living, may act as remote caufes
of confumption in two ways. 1ft, By inducing
general indirect debility, or 2dly, By propelling
fo much blood to the lungs as to excite an hemorr-
hage ; thus creating them a *weak* part, and thereby
rendering them in future lefs capable of refifting
the renewed action of one or many of the preced-

ing caufes. An hæmoptyfis was brought on a young
gentleman about nineteen years of age, of a delicate conftitution, from the exercife of riding forty
miles in a *ftage coach*, upon a warm day in the
month of Auguft laft.

A fudden ceffation of any ufual evacuation of
blood, and a neglect of periodical blood-letting,
are, with great propriety, confidered by writers
very frequent remote caufes of this difeafe. When
a ceffation of any of the fanguinary difcharges,
which I have mentioned, occur, from accident or
by *art*, the perfon is, in moft inftances, foon troubled with uneafinefs and oppreffion at the breaft,
accompanied with quick refpiration. In thefe inftances, unlefs fome evacuations are timely ufed,
or the ufual *difcharge* comes on, he is often attacked with a fpitting of blood, or fymptoms of phthifis. In perfons afflicted with a difcharge of blood
from the hæmorrhoidal veffels, great caution is re-
quifite in their treatment, left a complaint of the
breaft be induced. *Hippocrates*, long ago, faid,
" that in the cure of *bleeding piles*, of long ftanding, unlefs one be left running there is a danger of
a dropfy or a phthifis," and the truth of this apho-
rifm has been repeatedly experienced by medical
practitioners fince his time. It may not be improper, in this place, to infert the following fact. " A
man, *fifty* years of age, was accuftomed to have a

copious hæmorrhoidal difcharge, two or three times a year, but was in other refpects healthy. This evacuation being imprudently checked, he began to perceive a wonderful fluttering in his *pulfe*, and foon after a tenfion in his left flank, which afcended towards the breaft, and an hæmoptoe prefently followed. Notwithftanding various means were tried, the former periodical difcharge could never be reftored; but the fpitting of blood returned frequently with the fame fymptoms, and at laft he died of a phthifis." The above cafe, which is not a rare one in the annals of medicine, fufficiently evinces the danger of fuddenly reftraining cuftomary difcharges, even in *old* perfons: it fhould therefore be ftudioufly guarded againft in that period of *life*, when the lungs are more *naturally* fufceptible of difeafe.

A fudden difappearance of certain eruptions, will next be noticed. What induced me to fuppofe a ceffation of thefe eruptions, in certain conftitutions, to be a caufe of phthifis, was the following cafe, which I was informed of fometime fince. A man, about twenty-five years old, of a good conftitution, had a number of the above pimples upon his back and fhoulders, fince his nineteenth year. They would occafionally inflame a little: at which period, they produced a fenfation of itching and difcharged a watery fluid. From fome caufe, which I am ignorant of, they fuddenly left him, and in a few days he was taken with a more than ufual difficulty of breathing, after any exercife, and a fenfe of fulnefs in his breaft. In a day or two, he had a difcharge of blood from his lungs, for which fymptom he was bled twice. In three or four weeks he was again feized with the fame fymptoms, and immediately had himfelf bled, which produced the defired effect of preventing the hæmoptyfis. I do not know the refult of this cafe, as the man left Philadelphia a fhort time after. Van Swieten informs us, " that an acrid ferum frequently oozes from the heads of children and dries into a cruft: fometimes a like kind of diforder fpreads over the fkin:" he further remarks, " If this excretion be checked, either by accident or defign, the moft terrible diforders and convulfions are the confequence. Nay the lungs are frequently thence affected, and a phthifis brought on." From thefe circumftances, I think the cure of eruptions of long ftanding, fhould be attempted with more caution than is ufual upon fuch occafions.

A too *fedentary* life is the next caufe we will advert to. We are perfuaded no phyfician will be furprifed to fee this confidered as productive of the difeafe in queftion, although it be the *reverfe* of many of the caufes, which have been already mentioned. An abftraction of the *ftimulus* of exercife, together with hard ftudy and fitting up late at night, are fome of the moft frequent fources of confumption. We are not conftrained to perufe *medical books* in fearch of *folitary* proofs of the above pofition. For we *fee* this in a much more forcible manner, from the large number of young perfons of both *fexes* who are yearly deftroyed by their influence. A fedentary life, and alfo the want of that tone which is imparted to the lungs in *finging*, has been given as a reafon why the *ladies* of a certain religious denomination are oftener afflicted with this difeafe than *others*. A ceffation of the menfes may no doubt occafionally be a caufe of confumption : though I do not think it is as frequently the cafe, as is the opinion of many refpectable writers upon this fubject. We have the authority of an ancient writer* for afferting, " that coughs, obftructions, and fuppurations of the *lungs*, may arife from a *fuppreffion* of the *lochia.*

An immoderate ufe of tobacco is the laft caufe that I will confider. When this plant is made ufe of in the way of *fmoking* it is certainly very injurious to perfons of weak conftitutions, and to thofe alfo difpofed to confumption from other circumftances. In Dr. Rufh's 2d. Vol. he obferves, " I have feen a cafe of confumption in a *youth* of feventeen, from the fpitting produced by the intemperate ufe of fegars."

* *Hippocrates.*

It is ftill more detrimental to the body when *chewed;* as, from the continued *ftimulus,* it exerts upon the mouth and falivary glands, a great quantity of that fluid, fo neceffary to *digeftion* and the fubfequent nutrition of the fyftem, is wafted. And indeed, this mode of ufing it, appears to leffen the powers of the digeftive organs, to a greater degree than any other. May we not with propriety add, in a general manner, that thofe who are much addicted to thefe injurious practices, are alfo expofed to many of the other caufes of this difeafe? This remark applies more particularly to the *younger* part of *mankind.* From the united action of hard drinking, and the exceffive ufe of tobacco, what terrible effects upon the fyftem may not be expected?

All the *remote* caufes that have been enumerated, induce either direct or indirect *debility* in the *lungs.* This debility, conftitutes the *predifpofing* caufe of phthifis. That a *debility* is produced by their action, we prefume no one will now doubt; and if we attentively confider all the hiftories of confumption, we fhall invariably find, that a *debility* was induced in every cafe, prior to the attack of the difeafe. From this we eafily underftand why thofe who are expofed to the action of many of the remote caufes, at the fame time, are more certainly attacked with phthifis. That a pulmonary confumption cannot occur without *previous* debility, has been fo ably and clearly demonſtrated in another place* both by *reaſoning*, *analogy* and *faɛts*, that I deem it unneceſ-ſary to dwell longer upon this ſubjeɛt, but will pro-ceed to conſider the *exciting* cauſe.

The exciting cauſe, in all caſes of phthiſis, is ſtimulus. Any of thoſe *remote* cauſes, that pro-duce exceſſive aɛtion, may induce this complaint, when the ſyſtem is in a ſtate of prediſpoſition. Whether it be heat, great exerciſe, an intemperate life, or any *other* cauſe that excites phthiſis, they all aɛt in the ſame manner.

I now go on to the conſideration of the *proximate* cauſe. The firſt I ſhall notice, and which appears to have met with the approbation of moſt medical authors, is the one that was broached by *Morton*. The Doɛtor aſſerted, that phthiſis is occaſioned by the abſorption of pus, or purulent, acrid matter in the conſtitution, from abſceſſes or ulcers in the lungs. This doɛtrine has been refuted in a learned and ſatisfaɛtory manner by Dr. *Reid*, in his valua-ble work on this diſeaſe. The opinion of the ab-ſorption of *pus*, is declining daily: and when we conſider that pus poſſeſſes no acrimonious or corro-ſive property, we cannot be ſurpriſed at it. But even admitting its acrimony in conſequence of diſ-eaſe, ſince we poſſeſs ſo many inſtances of its being

* Ruſh's Works, 1ſt and 2d Vols.

in large quantities in the body, without inducing phthifis, we fhould be obliged to doubt the truth of this theory. Dr. *Reid*, " In one patient found three pints of pure pus in the pericardium without any ulcer on that membrane or on the heart ;" and, in another, he found " the cavity of the pleura, on the right fide, diftended with pus, the lungs compreffed into a very fmall compafs, but no appearance of an ulcer or erofion on thefe organs, or under the pleura." In neither of thefe inftances, and in *many* others that might be adduced, does pus appear to poffefs any acrid property—far from it : and from the various experiments* that have been made upon this *fluid*, we are confirmed in the opinion, that it is entirely devoid of *any* irritating power. In fuppurations of the *liver* and *kidneys*, when nearly their whole fubftance have been found in a ftate of *pus*, we do not perceive thofe phenomena that are attributed to the abforption of matter in phthifis ; but if, in any cafe, this difeafe could be produced by abforption of pus, we certainly fhould fee it in thofe inftances, where this fluid has exifted for fome time in the lungs themfelves ? This we do not find to be the cafe ; for there are innumerable inftances, in which pus has been expectorated, for a long period, without any fymptoms of confumption. This was the cafe, to a remarkable degree, in the fubfequent hiftory, which I tranfcribe from *Van Swieten's commentaries*, of a

* See *Home* on the properties of pus.

perfon of diftinction, who died upwards of *feventy*. " I faw him," fays the baron, " for more than four years previous to his death, fpit up, every morning, fome ounces of well digefted *pus*, with great eafe; and, during the reft of the day, he frequently fpat out the like matter. He folemnly affirmed he had fpit out a like quantity for *thirty years:* and this was confirmed by phyficians deferving of credit, who had known him long, and had frequently been confulted by him." What muft further increafe the opinion, that phthifis cannot be the confequence of abforbed pus, our *author* informs us, that the fubject of the above cafe " followed his ufual employments, and ufed a pretty high and plentiful diet."

The next caufes which I fhall hint at are *tubercles* and *ulcers* in the lungs. Thefe are fuppofed, by many writers and phyficians, to be frequent fources of this difeafe; but they appear to be as certainly the effect of previous difeafe in the lungs, as *fchirri* or *abfceffes* are, in any part of the animal fyftem. We might, with equal propriety, fuppofe a *fuppuration* of the liver, or a difcharge of water into the *ventricles* of the brain, to be the caufes of the *hepatic* or the *hydrochephalic ftates* of fever, as affert, tubercles or abfceffes in the lungs, to be caufes of pulmonary confumption. If we fuppofe an *ulcer* or *tubercle* to be the caufes of phthifis, how are we

to explain the appearance of its phenomena prior
to the exiftence of thefe fuppofed caufes? For
all cafes of phthifis are well marked before any
ulcer or tubercle can, with propriety, be fufpected
to be prefent. And further, the difeafe is formed,
in many cafes, for fome time before any pus, or
even mucus is coughed up.

I come now to offer a few remarks upon the theory of the *ingenious*, and juftly celebrated Dr. *Beddoes ;* and forry I am that to it I cannot fubfcribe.
I do not flatter myfelf with the idea of being able
to produce any new or fatisfactory objections to this
original and fimple theory of confumption ; but
fuch as they are, they appear in my own mind to
be conclufive. Dr. Beddoes, from remarking that
pregnancy fufpended this dreadful difeafe, and from
obferving the appearances of phthifical perfons, has
concluded a *fuper oxygenation* of the fyftem to be
the caufe of confumption. Although the Doctor has
advanced many arguments in favour of his hypo-
thefis, it appears unfatisfactory from the following
confiderations.

1ft, Pregnancy does not *uniformly* fufpend confumption. Dr. Rufh has communicated to me the
following cafe of a lady, whom he attended fome
years fince, in this difeafe. After having been afflicted with phthifis for fome time, fhe became

pregnant, and died in the fifth month of her geſta-
tion, without any viſible abatement of her phthiſical ſymptoms. I do not doubt of their being
many ſuch inſtances, though I am not acquainted
with them.

2dly, When a conception of *twins* has taken
place, we do not find the ſymptoms ſooner, or
to a greater degree relieved, than in caſes of common conception; which ſhould be the caſe agreea-
bly to this theory.

3dly, When pregnancy enſues the ſymptoms of
the diſeaſe are not abated in the progreſſive order,
that this theory would lead us to ſuppoſe. In other
words, their conſumptive ſymptoms are as much
relieved at the fifth or ſixth month, in ſome caſes,
as they are in the eighth or ninth.

4thly, In caſes of phthiſis, when a dropſy of the
abdomen has taken place, the oppreſſion and difficulty of reſpiration are evidently increaſed. In
this inſtance, " from the impeded action of the diaphragm," thoſe ſymptoms ſhould leſſen, as leſs
oxygine is received at each inſpiration.

5thly, Perſons with narrow and ſmall breaſts are
certainly much more liable to this diſeaſe than thoſe
who poſſeſs large and prominent cheſts. But this

should not be the cafe, if the Doctor's opinion was juft; for furely lefs *pure* air will be abforbed by the former than the latter.

6thly, As the Doctor was aware of the great difficulty of refpiration, in phthifical patients, when in crouded rooms, he anfwers this objection to his theory, by fuppofing that their " temperature may *counteract* the diminifhed proportion of oxygine:" this, however, appears to be unfatisfactory. Phthifical patients feem to fuffer much lefs from heat, when not ufing exercife, than perfons in health. Although the temperature of a room has certainly fome influence in aggravating the refpiration of confumptive perfons, yet when in fituations of the fame degree of heat, their breathing is not performed with fuch difficulty or uneafinefs to themfelves, as when in crouded apartments, particularly, where many lights are burning. The inhabitants of *cold* countries, fuffer little from pulmonary complaints. Is not this an objection to this theory, fince it is fuppofed, that in an equal volume of air, a greater proportion of oxygine exifts in cold, than hot countries? I will not advert to the acknowledged fact, that the difeafe we are confidering, is much more frequent in cities than in the country; though, believing the Doctor wrong when he fuppofes that *pure* air is in as great a quantity in each fituation. As probably the great difference, as to the manner of living, may explain why the inhabitants of the one fuffer more by this complaint. Neither will I bring forward, as an argument againft the Doctor's theory, the cafes in which oxygine gas has been afferted to be productive of beneficial effects in this difeafe; for even admitting thefe facts they do not prove any thing.

I have attempted, in another part of my piece, to collect together the different circumftances of the fyftem that have either fufpended or cured this difeafe, befides conception. It cannot be fuppofed, that *mania* and the other ftates of the body there enumerated, act by diminifhing oxygine. I do not know of a cafe, in which, from pregnancy fufpending the fymptoms of phthifis, they have not recurred after delivery. After confidering the nature of the different circumftances that have retarded the progrefs of confumption, they appear to produce this effect, either by tranflating the morbid excitement from the lungs to another part of the body, or by inducing, in a part or parts of the body, an action different from, or greater in violence, than the one in the this difeafed vifcus. I am not ignorant, however, that other ftates of difeafe have enfued without much relief to the fymptoms of phthifis. In the *medical repofitory*, vol. I. we find, that in a patient of Dr. *Crofwel*'s, after the pulmonary complaint had proceeded fo far that a regular cough, hectic, and expectoration of pus, had taken place: fhe was feized with a regular intermittent, which continued for two or three weeks without any very important abatement to the phthifical fymptoms. But we are alfo informed, that, " after the difappearance of the ague and fever, the confumptive fymptoms increafed in violence."

After having confidered the phenomena, caufes and cure of phthifis, I am difpofed to conclude, that a *morbid excitement* in the blood-veffels, generally, but efpecially in thofe of the lungs, is the proximate caufe of this difeafe. I have neither leifure nor abilities to offer any thing of my own upon this fubject; but have adopted the above, fince it appears to be the only one calculated to explain the different appearances of confumption.

I will now commence the confideration of the *cure* of confumption. This is the moft difficult part of my fubject, and, as in other inftances, alfo moft defirable.

It is a general obfervation, that difeafes are eafier avoided than cured; and this is applicable in a peculiar manner to this difeafe, which when confirmed, is acknowledged by moft phyficians to be generally fatal. It may be proper to advert to fome of the caufes that have led to the above conclufion and which can be affigned why it proves fo difficult of cure.

Motion certainly aggravates the difeafe, and increafes the difficulty of cure, in an inflamed part. This caufe operates in the moft ftriking manner in the prefent difeafe. Independent of the motion of the lungs, which cannot be avoided, when they are difeafed, this is evidently increafed, and they fuffer alfo from violent fits of coughing, which quickens the refpiration and alfo the determination of blood towards them. The continued motion of the lungs has been confidered by all writers as a caufe that retards the cure, and increafes the difeafes of this vifcus. Upon this fubject, Mr. *John Hunter* " thinks it a great pity that we do not accuftom ourfelves to move one fide of our thorax independent of the other, as we from habit move one eyelid independent of the other." Hence, if we could prevent the cough, and conftantly keep the refpiration nearly natural, in phthifical patients, it is more than conjecture, that this difeafe would be nearly in the fame ftate, and admit of a cure as *certainly*, and alfo as *readily*, as any internal part, in the fame inflamed fituation.

To the above, we may add another caufe; which, fince it refts with the patients themfelves, and as its imprudence has been fhewn by every writer upon this difeafe, it is not a little furprifing that it ftill continues. I mean that neglect of applying for *medical* aid, which is fo univerfal in this difeafe, until but a fmall profpect of fuccefs remains from the employment of any method of cure. Perfons having fymptoms of an incipient difeafe of the breaft, appear afhamed of confefling it to their friends; and when it cannot be avoided longer, and they do feek a phyfician, they ftill endeavour all in their power to convince him, their difeafe is any other than phthifis. We fometimes fee thefe patients unfortunately gain their point at the expenfe of their lives. This is not folely confined to the commencement of the difeafe. Dr. Rufh fays " I have never met with but one man; who, upon his being afked, what was the matter with him, anfwered unequivocally that he was in a confumption." Dr. Fothergill obferves, " We cannot, I think, be too induftrious in propagating, that the time at which a phyfician can be of the moft ufe, in the cure of comfumption, is at the firft beginning;" and he further obferves, that, " the flighteft catarrhal defluction, ought not to be neglected, if it does not go off in a few days." Every one will agree to the propriety of thefe obfervations. Is it not then a great misfortune, that neither of the truths they contain are often attended to? This feems to have ever been the cafe, fince all writers upon this difeafe complain they are not applied to in time. We should, therefore, not attribute the great fatality of phthisis to its being incurable : for the difficulty of cure of *every* form of disease, is increased or diminished in proportion to the time it has continued previous to the application of its remedies. Some of the most trifling diseases have, from neglect, often terminated in death. This being the case, we cannot be surprised to see consumption so frequently rendered incurable by negligence ; as it is a disease ever attended with great danger.

I will now proceed to the consideration of the remedies, after the formation of phthisis : and first of blood-letting.

Almost all authors recommend this remedy, to a certain degree, in this disease ; but it appears seldom to have been used sufficiently, as from the very epithet, which is applied to this form of disease, it has been supposed to require but little depletion, and hence in most writers we are desired to draw blood in *small* quantities, and to repeat it at certain intervals. This practice, I firmly believe, is the reason that many physicians are discouraged, and thus attribute their ill-success to the remedy they had so *sparingly* employed. At the first appearance of phthisis, this " noble remedy," should be used with great freedom, though directed with judgment. To what can we attribute the universal

fuccefs of practitioners in *pleurify*, but to their libe-
ral employment of the lancet? In this difeafe is
often drawn as much blood in a few days, as a
phthifical patient lofes in many months. This
practice appears to be directed rather by the " name
of the difeafe that the ftate of the fyftem," as I
have repeatedly feen patients in phthifis, whofe
fymptoms called as loudly for its ufe as pleurify
often does.

I would not wifh it concluded from this, that I
fhould draw as much blood, in the fame fpace of
time, from a perfon afflicted with confumption, as
from a pleuritic patient. This would not be neceffary,
as one or two large blood-lettings, together with
the ufe of other remedies, would probably ftop its
progrefs and prevent *tubercles* or *ulcers* taking
place. It is a fubject of much regret, that phyficians are feldom confulted until the above appearances are formed. But even when *ulcers* have been
formed, blood-letting may be ufed with much advantage to a greater extent than is ufually the cafe.
It is not folely from the good effects I have feen
follow this remedy, that I fuppofe larger quantities
are proper than are in moft cafes taken ; but Dr.
Mead obferves, " If the lungs be *ulcerated* and the
fever runs high, it will be proper to take away as
much blood as the patient can bear, at proper intervals." In the Edinburgh medical effays, vol. iv.

this remedy is fpoken of in high terms, by an *anonymous* writer, after *ulcers* have taken place. He fays, " as blood-letting takes off or confiderably abates the violence of the hectic fever, it may, in fact, be of no real expenfe at all; fince by this means, it prevents the great lofs of fluids by the colliquative fweats and diarrhea." In this ftate of phthifis, this remedy prevents the found parts being affected with inflamation, and thus, as it were, confines the difeafe to a fmall part of the lungs. It retards the formation of pus, and caufes the matter to be expectorated, with greater eafe; and alfo leffens the violence and frequency of the cough. Thus the patient is lefs harraffed by this diftreffing fymptom, and the ulcerated part of the lungs is lefs irritated than it would be, from much coughing and a difficult expectoration. I faw thefe effects follow the lofs of *fix* ounces of blood, in an Irifh gentleman, a few weeks before his death. I was particular in my inquiries, and found he had expectorated with lefs difficulty than ufual; and that no pain had fucceeded his exertions in coughing, which had hitherto been the cafe. He alfo flept more the enfuing night, and found himfelf in the morning refrefhed to a greater degree than he had been for fome time.

We are to be guided with refpect to the quantity of blood to be drawn and its repetition, by the *fymp-*

toms, *pulfe*, and the *appearance* of the blood. Relief fucceeding this remedy is certainly a fure indication of the propriety of its ufe. But this not immediately taking place, fhould never deter us from its renewed application in this difeafe. It does not in other difeafes, nor with other remedies, and neither fhould it in this. Blood-letting is often repeated in other ftates of difeafe, when if phyficians had been regulated in its ufe, folely from its *apparent* beneficial effects, its further ufe would have been confidered injurious. We do not in the *fcarlalina*, or *intermitting* fever lay afide the exhibition of *emetics* and the *bark*, becaufe one or two dofes do not cure thefe difeafes: and experience confirms the opinion that venefection in phthifis is not to be deferted merely from its ufe not being attended with immediate good effects. I have often witneffed the fymptoms of this difeafe abating after the fecond or third blood-letting, when they appeared to be rather increafed by the firft ufe of this remedy. The conftitution of the patient fhould have fome influence in judging of the propriety of this remedy; though we would not be directed by this confideration alone. The following fymptoms feem to indicate its neceffity : much pain ; or a fenfation of heat or fulnefs in the cheft ; a hard, flow, much increafed, or irregular pulfe; and blood appearing in the expectoration. To which may be added, very difficult breathing, at the commencement of the difeafe.

Blood drawn in this difeafe feldom exhibits any *fize*, but ufually a more inflamatory appearance. That blood deftitute of this fizy or buffy coat, as it is termed, is an indication of a greater inflamatory diathefis than when prefent, has been fatisfactory fhewed in a late valuable publication.* Daily obfervation proves, that this appearance of the blood does not take place till towards the clofe of acute difeafes, after their violence have been reduced by depleting remedies. A want of *fizinefs* is not unfrequent even in the clofe of confumption.

It was formerly obferved, that the menfes fometimes continued regular during the greater part of this difeafe. When this is the cafe, or fhould in any period of the difeafe a difcharge of blood from the nofe or any other parts take place, blood-letting is neceffary; and no efforts fhould be made to ftop thefe difcharges unlefs profufe. *Bennet*, who had the beft experience in this difeafe, being both patient and phyfician, remarks, that " all confumptive perfons who have frequent moderate bleedings at the *nofe* hold out the longer for this difcharge." This remark of our *author* is ftrictly true, and moft perfons who have had much practice in this difeafe, have made the fame obfervation. Dr. *Rufh* has feen " two cafes of inflamatory confumption, attended by an hæmorrhage of a *quart* of blood from the

* Rufh's 4th Vol.

lungs; they both recovered to the great joy and fur-
prife of all connected with them."

When we fee phthifical cafes thus unufually protracted or cured by accidental difcharges of blood,
is it not more than theoretical to expect greater advantages muft enfue from the timely and juaicious
employment of this remedy? Surely we fhould
not wait for a natural effufion of blood, depending
upon various circumftances, but procure this difcharge when there are moft profpects of relief, and
no danger to the patient? From this we will poffefs
two advantages, that are abfolutely neceffary to en-
fure the moft beneficial confequences from phle-
botomy. I mean a proper time and the proper quantity. We never fee a natural difcharge of blood
take place, at the time we would expect the moft
falutary effects; and likewife neither too great or
too fmall in quantity. It may poffibly be thought
a rafh practice, fays Dr. *Mead,* to draw blood, even
when the patient is much wafted in his flefh, and
very weak; but this great phyfician obferves, that
" a temporary leffening of the ftrength is of fervice
when attended with a part of the caufe, which
would weaken the body more and more every day."
The Doctor adds, " I have feen cafes judged almoft defperate, where this method of practice fucceeded well."

I knew the case of a lady, among many of a similar nature, whose disease was protracted for years by the judicious use of bleeding, by my worthy *preceptor ;* and I have every reason to conclude she would have perfectly recovered if he had been consulted in time.

When in females conception suspends phthisis, may not the use of this remedy be attended with great prospects of success in preventing its recurrence? While upon this subject I will digress and observe, that it appears to be a bad practice to *discontinue* the use of remedies in this disease, when suspended by pregnancy. Does n)t this interval afford the best opportunity for the application of our remedies? Before quitting the subject of blood-letting, as a remedy in the cure of phthisis, I would add, that it has been given as an argument against its use, that all consumptive patients are so reduced as but little blood remains in the body. That this is not the case, appears by the following from *Morgagni*. " It must not be passed over in silence, that in a consumptive woman, in whom, by reason of the very emaciated state of her whole body, the skin seemed scarcely to adhere to her very thin bones, the lungs when cut into, poured out a large quantity of blood mixed with sanies :" I must also add, that in two other patients (one of whom had expectorated pus) both of them had a great quan-

tity in their ulcerated and putrid lungs, notwithftanding they had difcharged a vaft quantity of blood
from their mouths and noftrils; and the fecond of
them, moreover, from all parts by which hæmorr-
hages happen, and that the carcafe of the fecond,
neverthelefs, fhewed in the left kidney a great ftag-
nation of blood, and in the *lumbar* region, had the
fanguiferous veffels very tumid and inflamed; and
that the blood-veffels of the firft were very turgid
with blood, in the *omentum, ftomach,* and *mefentery.*"

I will next fay a few words upon purgatives.
This clafs of medicines appears to have been too
much neglected, in the treatment of confumption.
The great objection, that has been confidered as
valid againft their employment, feems to be, that
a purging occurs in the laft ftage of the difeafe, and
often haftens its fatal termination. This however
fhould have no weight; for, in the beginning of the
malady, the patient is coftive, which fymptom we
know has a tendency to increafe his complaint.
Moreover, fince we uniformly perceive fuch immediate good effects to follow a diarrhea, though occurring when phthifis is far advanced, we muft expect much greater in an earlier period. In moft difeafes the ftate of the alimentary canal has much influence upon the refpiration of the patient; but in
this, it produces remarkable effects; and we find
this fymptom to be hurried or relieved according to

the ftate of the bowels. Some of thofe medicines, that have been confidered as fpecifics in phthifis, appear to have produced their good effects by in-ducing a relaxed ftate of the inteftines. *Bennet* fpeaks favourably of gentle laxatives, in the beginning of the difeafe, and appears to have experienced advan-tages from them. The body, in the incipient ftage, or previoufly to confumption progreffing much, fhould always be kept open ; but I think medicines of the more ftimulating clafs of purgatives are to be preferred for this purpofe.

Much has been written to fhew the great advan-tages that are derived from *emetics* by Doctors *Reid*, *Simmons* and others, in the cure of confumption. But, as from the general operation of thefe medi-cines, they feem to act very powerfully upon the lungs, inducing a great determination of blood to them, fo that a fpitting of blood might be appre-hended, or at leaft a recurrence of this fymptom, if the patient had been afflicted with it, their em-ployment feems very doubtful ; at leaft in the begin-ning of the complaint they muft prove injurious. After the formation of large abfceffes, the ufe of gentle vomits may be attended with temporary re-lief to the patient's fufferings ; and when fo large a quantity of matter exifts in the lungs, that a fuffo-cation is threatened, they are certainly to be em-ployed, The continued ufe of thefe medicines for

months, and repeated daily, have, in the hands of
fome refpectable phyficians, been followed by fuccefs. Dr. *Marryat*, in his *New practice of phyfic*,
fpeaks much in praife of, and prefcribes with freedom,
what are called *dry vomits*, from their operation
not being promoted by drinking, as is ufually the
cafe. The emetic, Dr. *Marryat* ufed, confifted of
the *fulphate* of copper and tart. emetic. I do not
know however if any peculiar good effects have
been afcertained by practitioners from this mode of
adminiftering vomits in phthifis. I will conclude
the fubject of emetics by obferving, that, in the
firft ftage of phthifis, they are detrimental, and in
an advanced they can be only *palliatives ;* but as
fuch, are never to be difregarded.

Sweating medicines have been employed, to a
fmall degree, and with fome perfons are faid to
have proved of fervice in this difeafe. We feldom
fee patients at that ftage of phthifis, in which *fudo-
rifics* would be of moft advantage, and even then
the *milder* fubftances of this clafs are preferable.

Too much cannot be faid of the beneficial effects of
bliffers, as a remedy in phthifis. They have been
recommended by nearly all writers upon this difeafe, and their repeated application is advifed.
A continued *bliffer* upon the breaft has, in numberlefs inftances, been evidently of great benefit to

perfons advanced in phthifis. Blifters however have, in moft cafes, been referved to the latter periods of phthifis; but this appears to be an improper practice; if any *permanent* advantages are to be expected from their application, they fhould be employed as foon as poffible : for can their ufe ever effect a *cure* when large abfceffes are already formed in the lungs ? I think great benefit would arife from the perpetual *irritation* of a blifter upon the fyftem, in an early ftage of phthifis. I am fenfible that the fear of increafing the inflammatory diathefis, will be the only objection that can be advanced, with any appearance of plaufibility, againft this mode of employing blifters in this malady. But even fhould this often be the cafe, fince we have in our poffeffion the means of reducing it, at pleafure, by depleting remedies, and when we will eventually derive fuch benefit by their employment, in this ftage of confumption, it is affuredly juftifiable to rifque this *tranfitory* evil. The way to obtain the beft effects of blifters, in phthifis, appears to be by alternately applying them to different parts of the body. Thus : as foon as a blifter upon one part appears to have loft its power, it fhould be fuffered to heal, but another be applied to a different place. By this, thofe parts that have been previoufly irritated, will in a fhort fpace of time, recover their ufual excitability, and again will produce the former good effects when blifters are *renewed*. I am

fure, more advantages will follow the above method
than can be expected from a *perpetual* blifter upon
any *one* part or parts of the fyftem. Thefe *ftimulating* applications feem to produce their effects, in
confumption, only by inducing a great degree of
excitement upon the furface of the body. In moft
difeafes, when *blifters* induce a *ftrangury*, they are
productive of greater advantages, than when this
effect does not follow their application : and indeed,
in fome difeafes, *cantharides* have been exhibited,
internally, fuccefsfully with this intention. I am not
able to fay with any degree of certainty whether
in confumption the fame effect has been obferved,
when fuch an occurrence takes place.

With refpect to *fetons* and *iffues*, which have
been much extolled by certain writers, I have but
little to fay. I have feldom feen them ufed and never with any lafting or remarkable effects.

Opium has been but fparingly ufed in the firft periods of confumption ; and this practice appears perfectly juft. As the operation of this medicine feems
now to be well underftood, we could not but expect
deleterious refults from the early ufe of fuch a pow-
erful ftimulant. In the latter part of this difeafe,
however, when the patient is afflicted with an incef-
fant cough, diarrhea, and other diftreffing fymptoms,
this medicine fhould be reforted to, fince it often

contributes to alleviate the agonies of death, and affords the unhappy fufferer an interval of eafe.

The *bark* has been adminiftered by many phyfi-cians in confumption. From this medicine produc-ing fuch wonderful effects in *intermitting* fevers, practitioners were led to expect the fame advantages in the cure of the hectic; and hence the bark has been tried in every period of this difeafe, to a very great extent. *Default*, many years ago, afferted, that this remedy did harm in difeafes of the lungs. Dr. *Fothergill* has known the bark often produce hæmoptyfis and other dangerous fymptoms, when adminiftered early in the difeafe, and " In the fub-fequent ftages, often indeed with lefs appearance of injury, but at leaft without benefit." *Torti* found the ufe of this medicine to be often attended with a manifeft abatement of the ufual paroxyfms of fever, but this effect foon ceafed, and the complaint pur-fued its natural courfe. Dr. *Mead*, treating of the efficacy of the bark in *fevers*, obferves, that, " it is pernicious alfo in thofe hectics, which are accompanied with ulcers of any of the *internal* parts." From the teftimony of refpectable writers, upon the ufe of the bark in phthifis, and from our own obfervation, we may conclude, that its em-ployment is certainly injurious in the earlier, and of no real benefit in the latter periods of the difeafe.

From the *elixir* of *vitriol* having performed a cure, in a certain cafe of confumption, when an undue dofe was taken by miftake, this medicine much excited the attention of phyficians. But notwithftanding its adminiftration has been, in many cafes, conducted with care, yet it has never realized the expectations that were formed of its powers in phthifis.

Balfamic medicines have been much employed in all cafes of difeafes of the breaft. I do not know any thing of their effects in cafes of confumption, having but feldom feen them ufed in this difeafe. As, in general, the articles of this clafs are evidently ftimulants, and from the obfervations on this fubject by many experienced perfons, I am fatisfied, their employment muft be improper in nearly all cafes. Dr. Fothergill, who has left us an excellent paper upon the ufe of *balfams*, in confumption, after afferting, that the *momentum* of the blood towards the lungs is increafed during its whole duration, obferves, " and as the medicines above mentioned, have a tendency, fome more fome lefs, according to the different degrees of activity, to increafe this *momentum*, ought we not to be extremely diffident in applying them in fuch cafes, by *whatever* authority they are mentioned ?"

In the London medical tranfactions, vol. 3, Dr.

Darwin relates the cafe of a young man, who was cured of this difeafe by the ufe of the *digitalis pur-purea.* This patient took one large fpoonful of the *decoction* twice a day, without the employment of any other medicine, and continued this for the fpace of fix weeks.

It appears by an ingenious and valuable effay* that the *rhus radicans* has been employed in feveral cafes of this difeafe. In one perfon who had been afflicted with confumption for two years, a ftrong *decoction* of its leaves much abated his pulmonary fymptoms. In the cafe of an aged woman, in whom fmall dofes of the *extract* evidently relieved her complaint, it produced this effect, in the opinion of the patient, by keeping her bowels open. And in a young man, in whom this medicine relieved the pain in his breaft, it " produced an *eruption* on the fkin, a flight *falivation*, and opened the bowels."

In thofe cafes of phthifis, attended with a difcharge of blood from the lungs, the exhibition of cooling laxatives, together with the ufe of *common falt*, and *nitre*, have, in many cafes, contributed in protracting the fatal termination of the difeafe.

* An inaugural differtation on the *rhus vernix*, &c. &c. By *Thomas Horsfield*.

I

I muſt not quit this part of my ſubject without obſerving, that the employment of *mercury* ſo as to produce a *ſalivation*, has been recommended as a remedy for phthiſis; and its uſe has in ſome caſes produced ſalutary effects. "I have found it difficult to produce a ſalivation in this diſeaſe. In one caſe it was ſucceeded with complete ſuccefs: but I am in doubt whether to attribute this cure to the mercury or to ſix *bleedings* which were alſo employed."* I will quit this head by obſerving, that it ſeems improbable to expect ſuccefs from this remedy, if employed, in the latter ſtages of conſumption.

Upon the ſubject of *pneumatic* medicine, in this diſeaſe, I cannot ſay much. Many phyſicians have employed a diminiſhed proportion of *pure* air, and have experienced various reſults. Dr. *Beddoes*, in his publication informs us, that he has obtained very great advantages, in a large number of caſes, by making his patients reſpire an atmoſphere in which the *oxygenous* part was leſſened: and we muſt alſo add, that the Doctor to prove his theory of conſumption, with much intrepidity endeavoured to induce upon himſelf this diſeaſe by breathing an *undue* quantity of pure air, which was attended with ſuccefs. Dr. *Girtanner*'s† trials prove, that the *car-*

* Ruſh's Lectures.

† Vol. I. *Medical* repoſitory.

bonic acid gas is of great service in some cases, use-
less in some, and sometimes hurtful. Dr. *Percival*
has administered *fixed* air to more than *thirty* patients in phthisis. He has seen cases in which the
hectic was abated, but its use has not, in one in-
stance, effected a cure " although the use of *Ne-
phetic air* was accompanied with proper internal remedies." But Dr. *Whethering* appears to have been
more successful in his trials. Dr. *Rush* in his lectures informed us, that from the authority of a re-
spectable physician,* lately from England, who had
repeatedly seen *phlogisticated* air administered, in
consumption, its employment was without success;
for though it always relieved for a time, its salutary
effects never continued long. It may be consider-
ed improper to omit mentioning that an *undue*
quantity of oxygine has, in many instances of
phthisis, produced very salutary effects. *Chaptal*
relates a striking case in proof of this, in a *gentleman* far advanced in the complaint.

An increased quantity of *pure air*, appears to be
only applicable to the latter, and a *diminished* proportion to the incipient periods of consumption.
Hence we may perhaps account for the contradic-
tory success of *pneumatic* medicine. I will add,
that, in one case, I attempted the use of oxygenous
gas in a phthisical patient, whose disease was much

* Dr. *Jardine*

advanced. In this perfon the action of the lungs was fo far impaired, that he could refpire but a fmall quantity of the air, yet his refpiration, and other fymptoms, were evidently relieved for one or two hours. Thefe appearances however I cannot attribute to the agency of the *air*, fince his expectorations were much excited, and his fpirits increafed from profpects of fuccefs by its employment.

As, fomewhat connected with this part of our fubject, I will juft obferve, that Dr. *Pearfon*, of Birmingham, England, has adminiftered the *vapour* of *vitriolic æther*, with great fuccefs, in confumption. The Doctor fays, " the *firft effects* of this application, are an agreeable fenfation of coolnefs in the cheft, an abatement of the dyfpnœa and cough, and after ten minutes or a quarter of an hour, eafier expectoration :" and that the " *ultimate effects* are, a removal of the local inflammation, a cleanfing and healing of the ulcerated lungs, and a fuppreffion of the hectic fever."*

A remedy recommended by fome, as a *fpecific* in confumption, is the earth bath. Van Swieten, in his commentaries on *Boerhaave*, tells us, that in fome parts of *Spain*, they have a method of curing phthifis, by the ufe of this remedy; and he quotes *Solano De Luque*, celebrated for his book

* Medical repofitory.

upon the *pulse*, in confirmation of this practice. *Solano* fpeaks of the *banos de tierra*, or earth baths, as a very old and common remedy in *Granada* and fome parts of *Andilufia*, in cafes of confumption; and relates feveral inftances of their good effects in his own practice. Dr. *Fouquet*, an ingenious French phyfician, has tried this remedy in two cafes. In one, a confirmed phthifis, he was un-fuccefsful; but the remedy had not a fair trial. In the fecond cafe, he was more fortunate: the pati-ent, a girl of eleven years old, was entirely reftored. A phyfician at *Warfaw* has likewife prefcribed the earth bath with good fuccefs in cafes of hectic fe-ver. This remedy was of late extenfively employed in England by a celebrated empiric, in confumptive cafes. In moft inftances it produced a very great fenfation of cold to the patient, " and we have not heard of any phthifical cafes in which good effects were decidedly obtained from it."*

I will now confider the different modes of ufing *exercife* in this difeafe. It is ufual, upon this occa-fion, to produce the opinion of the great *Sydenham*, who afferted, that riding on *horfeback* was as certain a cure for confumption as the *bark* for intermitting fever. This I believe; but as there is a certain time when the bark would do harm in the fever, fo alfo is there a period when riding would as cer-

* The American Encyclopædia.

tainly prove injurious to the phthifical patient,
Moft writers advife the employment of this exercife
in the difeafe we are confidering ; but it is proper to
be regulated in its ufe by the condition of the fyftem,
as much fo, as in *prefcribing* any other remedy. In
many perfons this exercife has proved beneficial in
one period, and detrimental in another ftage of the
difeafe. When in the after part of the day the
pulfe becomes more frequent, accompanied with
heat and other feverifh fymptoms, this exercife
would certainly increafe the difeafe. As riding on
horfeback agitates the *vicera* and determines the
circulation towards the lungs more than riding in a
carriage or *walking*, either of the latter would in
many cafes be preferable to begin with.

The exercife and fatigue of a *camp* life has in
many inftances proved a cure to this difeafe.

Sailing has been ftrongly recommended in confumption ; and Dr. *Gilcrift* has repeatedly experienced the moft *extraordinary* advantages from this
remedy in cafes of phthifis. That the good effects of
failing are produced by the *change* of air, the *motion*,
and the *vomiting* have been *each* embraced, as opi-
nions, by different authors. Perhaps we may with
more propriety conclude that all thefe circumftances
are concerned, in the production of the advantages,
that have followed long *fea voyages.*

Another mode of uſing exerciſe has lately been highly extolled in this diſeaſe, by Dr. *James Charmichael Smith*, in his account of the effects of *ſwinging*, employed as a remedy in the pulmonary conſumption and hectic fever. Dr. Smith refers the ſalutary effects of ſea voyages entirely to the peculiar motion which is connected with ſailing. By *motion* Dr. Smith means ſuch action as is not neceſſarily accompanied with any agitation of the body, and which is totally independent of *muſcular* exertion; upon theſe grounds he was induced to believe that the *motion* produced in *ſwinging* would prove at leaſt as beneficial in phthiſical caſes as *ſailing*. This opinion the Doctor ſays, experience has verified, and ſucceſs has followed its uſe in many inſtances.

I ſhall conclude this part of my diſſertation with a few general remarks upon the diet and regulation, neceſſary for conſumptive patients. It appears to be admitted, on all ſides, that a low diet is beſt calculated to contribute in the cure of this diſeaſe.*

* We may remark, that the diet of perſons in conſumption does not ſeem to be as ſtrictly attended to as it deſerves, or appears to have been by phyſicians of former times. The old writers in moſt caſes depended *more* upon the proper regulation of the patient, relative to this, than any thing elſe. *Diocles* directed his patients to refrain from *animal* food, and even ſays, that nothing is of any conſequence without *abſtinence*. We may add alſo of this phyſician, that he likewiſe directed ſweats, ſince they neceſſarily *took away ſtrength*.

A vegetable diet feems to be neceffary in the incipient ftage of phthifis, though a *little animal* food
may be allowed to fome patients in this period of
the difcafe. A certain proportion of *falt meat* has
advantageoufly conftituted a part of the animal food
of many perfons in an advanced ftage of confumption. .

Milk has long been confidered as peculiarly
adapted to this difeafe; though we may obferve
it has often increafed the malady from patients ima-
gining that while living upon this article of diet it
was impoffible to go to an excefs in its ufe. In moft
patients a diet of milk and vegetables feem to leffen
fufficiently the inflammatory diathefis, and its long
continued ufe, together with a temperate life and
other remedies, have in numerous cafes been followed by complete fuccefs. The milk obtained from
moft animals may be employed, but that of the *non-
ruminants* is fuppofed to be beft fuited to cafes of
phthifis. The ufe of *whey* has often produced thofe
advantages that are derived from a milk diet to a
greater degree, and its employment has frequently
been fuccefsful.

Since moft ripe fruits are cooling and prove laxative, their ufe fhould be encouraged, as they appear
well fitted to cafes of this difeafe. Dr. *Hoffman* has
the cafe of a youth, who, after being far advanced in

this difeafe, was cured by eating a large quantity of *garden ftrawberries.* Dr. *Moore** relates two cafes of patients in phthifis, that appeared to be cured by living, for fome time, almoft entirely upon ripe *grapes;* and Dr. Rufh in his lectures fays, he has alfo feen one cure, by the ufe of this fruit. *Tulpius* relates the cafe of a woman, in an emaciated and low ftate of confumption, who was cured by a diet of *raw oysters* which fhe eat greedily. It is fuppofed, and with much probability, that in the many cafes of this difeafe related as cured by grapes and other particular fubftances, the patients were not afflicted with true phthifis.†

Sugar, as a part of the diet of perfons in this malady, particularly in the incipient period, has been advifed by fome phyficians: and this fubftance does not appear to be improper, at any time, unlefs the diarrhœa be prefent.

Mucilage, from its affording nourifhment without heating the fyftem, has been recommended with great propriety as the diet of phthifical patients.

With refpect to fpirituous liquors, it is only neceffary to obferve, that they fhould never be ufed;

* A view of fociety and manners in Italy, by John Moore, M. D. Vol. I.

† Barton's Lectures.

cooling acidulous drinks or pure water being only proper in phthifis.

Perfons in confumption, fhould be particular in keeping regular hours, avoiding the night air, and exercife before they have breakfafted, and if poffible, fpending the winter feafon in cold climates. Their drefs muft be warmer than the feafon may feem to require, and flannel is proper to be always worn next to the body both in *winter* and *fummer*.

After having collected together, in as concife a manner as poffible, what appears to be moft important in the *hiftory, caufes* and *cure* of phthifis, before clofing my differtation, I will add alfo a few words relative to its prevention.

Since perfons difpofed to this difeafe by a certain form of the body, and thofe whofe *anceftors* have been afflicted with it, are moft ufually its fubjects : the following obfervations will, in a more particular manner, allude to them. Perfons *thus* circumftanced, fhould be careful to avoid all the caufes that have been confidered as having a tendency to increafe or create a predifpofition to pulmonic affections.

When too great a determination of blood to the breaft is obferved, or any fymptoms of an hæmop-

tyfis take place, which in thofe predifpofed to phthifis, often occurs as early as the fixteenth year, fuch
perfons fhould be confidered as being very danger-
oufly fituated, and thefe firft fymptoms of a predifpofition to phthifis are never to be difregarded. In
the above cafes, occafional bleeding, moderate
diet, and exercife, a temperate life, and the proper
ufe of the cold bath, will prevent the difeafe.

At the beginning of fummer, many young perfons are fubject to a bleeding at the nofe. We
fhould be careful of ftopping this difcharge in every
cafe, but more fo in thofe difpofed to the difeafe in
queftion. I will now ftate a cafe from *Bennet.*
" A youth, who had received a confumptive habit
from his parents, and who neverthelefs enjoyed
almoft uninterrupted health from his fixteenth to his
twenty-fifth year, by means of a bleeding at the
nofe. For, towards the end of fpring, and almoft
through the whole fummer, *once* or *twice* a *day*, he
bled from the nofe an *ounce* or fometimes *two ounces*
of blood; at twenty-five this hæmorrhage ftopped,
on his taking cold in his head: foon after his breaft
began to be overcharged, and a hæmoptoe, and
other fymptoms of phthifis followed; the lancet was
ufed but with little fuccefs: but a *copious* hæmorrhage returning, the breaft grew firm and he efcap-
ed fo great danger without any other confiderable
alteration in his health." This fact is valuable in

two refpects; it firft fhews that although a periodical difcharge, in perfons predifpofed to phthifis,
be rather great and alfo frequent, yet much caution
is neceffary in reftraining it, and alfo teaches us
that when an hæmorrhage does not return and
dangerous fymptoms follow, that together with
bleeding and other remedies, we fhould draw
blood artificially from the part, if this be pradti-
cable.

I cannot refrain from making one remark upon
Bennet's cafe. Since we are informed that a *copious*
flow of blood from the nofe relieved the youth after he had ineffedtually ufed the lancet, it only
proves it had been too fparingly employed.

Perhaps it may be faid that I am too *fanguine* upon the advantages of blood-letting, either natural
or artificial, in preventing phthifis. But to fhew
the great efficacy of this remedy in preventing the
difeafe, I fhall make ufe of the following cafe, in
which the difpofition to a confumption was very
great; and we may add, the *author** from whom
it is taken cannot be accufed of being very partial
to this remedy in phthifis. "A robuft, healthy
man married a beautiful young lady, in whofe family this difeafe was hereditary. Of this marriage
were born *four* children, three of whom died of

true phthifis: the fourth and laft, terrified by the fate of the reft, prevented, by *frequent* and *copious* bleeding, the hæmoptoe. He died about *forty* of a dropfy. This man had feveral children, none of whom were afflicted with any diforder of the lungs, through a courfe of years more numerous than thofe of their fathers ; and happy in a healthy off-fpring, of whom fome are grown up to manhood, perfectly well."

If, in the one cafe, a periodical difcharge of blood, and in the other, a long *continued* ufe of *venefection*, produced fuch great effects in perfons liable to confumption, in that manner which all phy-ficians fuppofe to be the moft difficult of prevention, may we not pofitively look for greater when pro-perly employed ?

Blood drawn from the hæmorrhoidal veffels is of benefit in preventing any fatal confequences from a ceffation of the *bleeding piles ;* and from its falu-tary effect in the enfuing cafe, I fhould be induced to ufe this remedy in a fimilar fituation. *Duretus* informs us, that when paft *fifty* he was troubled with a frequent and copious difcharge of blood from the lungs, in confequence of a hæmorrhage from his nofe, to which he was fubject, being *fup-preffed*, but was perfectly recovered by the applica-tion of *leeches* to the *hæmorrhoidal* veffels.

Thofe who are fo unfortunate as to be predifpofed to confumption from any caufe whatever,
fhould ever bear in mind, that when once induced,
this malady

> " ———— every moment grows,
> And gains new ftrength and vigour as it goes."

I will clofe thefe remarks refpecting the prevention of phthifis, with the following quotation from
Melmont's *Cicero* on old age : " To this end we
fhould be regularly attentive to the article of health;
ufe moderate exercife, and neither eat nor drink
more than is neceffary for repairing our ftrength,
without oppreffing the organs of digeftion."

Having now concluded my obfervations upon
confumption, I wifh *each* profeffor of this univerfity,
to accept of my acknowledgments, for the great
opportunities of improvement, I have had in their
refpective branches. I wifh, however, to return my
thanks in a particular manner to Dr. Barton, profeffor of the materia medica and botany, for the
attention and politenefs I have received from him.

I beg, alfo, Dr. Charles Caldwell to receive my
thanks, for the advice he has given me in many
parts of my medical purfuits; having refided in
the fame houfe during the greater part of that period.

www.ingramcontent.com/pod-product-compliance
Lightning Source LLC
Chambersburg PA
CBHW022142090426
42742CB00010B/1357